MW01173872

The Exemplar and Role Model for Mankind

Imam al-Jawad

By:

The Religious Authority

Grand Ayatollah al-Sayyid Mohammed Taqi al-Modarresi

أهل البيت

HOUSEHOLD
PUBLICATIONS

بسم الله الرحمن الرحيم

In the Name of Allah, the Compassionate the Merciful

Transliteration

Arabic terms which do not have standard spellings in English have been transliterated according to the system set out on this page.

ء	a, i, or u (initial form)	ل	l
ء	ʾ (medial or final form)	م	m
ا	a	ن	n
ب	b	ه	h
ت	t	و	w
ث	th	ي	y
ج	j	ة	h (without *iḍāfah*)
ح	ḥ	ة	t (with *iḍāfah*)
خ	kh	∼	∼
د	d	ال	al- *
ذ	dh	ـَ	a
ر	r	ـِ	i
ز	z	ـُ	u
س	s	ـا / آ / ى	ā
ش	sh	ـِي	ī
ص	ṣ	ـُو	ū
ض	ḍ	آ	ʾā (medial form)
ط	ṭ	ـَيْ	ay
ظ	ẓ	ـَيّ	ayy
ع	ʿ	ـِيّ	iyy (medial form)
غ	gh	ـِيّ	ī (final form)
ف	f	ـَوْ	aw
ق	q	ـَوّ	aww
ك	k	ـُوّ	uww

* This does not apply, however, to those Arabic parts of the text that in practice are meant to be articulated verbally. See the fourth convention mentioned in the Translator's Preface.

Contents

Introduction

Praise be to Allah, who guides His servants to His obedience, and who ordains goodness in their worship. May peace and blessings be upon the Prophet Muḥammad, the master of the messengers, and upon his infallible family.

It is a pleasure for me to find an opportunity to immerse my humble pen in the sea of heroism and genius that characterizes the life of Imam al-Jawād ('a), the ninth of the pure Imams, where heroism merges with integrity, and purity with glory and honor.

Imam al-Jawād ('a), whose blessed life I am honored to briefly recount, was the shortest-lived of the Imams, passing away at a young age. He was born in the year 195 AH and passed away in the year 220 AH, making his life span only 25 years. This brief lifespan makes his life a subject of significant interest, inviting more detailed study, particularly as some people may find it surprising that a young boy of only seven years could be an Imam.

Furthermore, the era of Imam al-Jawād, peace be upon him, was rich with various events and different developments, making it a period worthy of special study. As we present the life of the Imam, we will also review some of the historical events that accompanied his life between the years 195 and 220 AH.

Here begins the detailed account, offering a thorough and comprehensive examination of events.

Chapter One

Noble Origin and Blessed Birth

1. His Father:

His father was Imam ʿAlī b. Musa b. Jaʿfar b. Muḥammad b. ʿAlī b. al-Ḥusayn b. ʿAlī b. Abī Ṭālib, peace be upon them. An extraordinary man whose virtue and knowledge filled the horizons of the Islamic world, praised by his opponents and hailed by his followers alike. He was the Riḍā (the one chosen by Allah), the Imam and the proof for the people, the leader and the exemplar.

2. His Mother:

His mother was Lady Sabīka the Nubian[1], who came to Medina with others from Africa. She joined the family of the Prophet and gave birth to their leader, Imam al-Jawād (ʻa). Some traditions suggest that she was from the people of Maria the Copt, the wife of the noble Prophet (peace be upon him and his family), though this is unlikely.

3. His Birth:

According to our belief, the Imam chosen by Allah to be a righteous role model must be perfect in every way. Any deficiency or flaw in thought or body indicates that the person is not an Imam. Imam

---

1. The Nubians are an ethnic group indigenous to the region of Nubia, located along the Nile River, which straddles the southern part of Egypt and the northern part of Sudan. Historically, Nubia was home to some of Africa's earliest civilizations, including the Kingdom of Kush, and has a rich cultural heritage that dates back thousands of years.

al-Riḍā (ʻa) had reached the age of fifty-five without having any children, which led some of the Wāqifiyya, who claimed the occultation of Imam Musa al-Kāẓim (peace be upon him) and denied the existence of any subsequent Imam, to spread rumors that Imam Al-Riḍāʾ was childless, a clear flaw in a religious leader. Hence, according to their claim, he could not be the true Imam. Some even wrote to him questioning his Imamate due to his lack of offspring, to which he replied: "How do you know that I will not have a son? By Allah, the days and nights will not pass before Allah grants me a son who will distinguish between truth and falsehood."[1]

A man once asked him, "Who is the Imam after you?"

He replied, "My son."

The man then said, "Can anyone claim he has a son without actually having one?"

The narrator reports that soon after, Abū Jaʿfar al-Jawād (ʻa) was born.[2]

Ibn Qiyām al-Wāsiṭī, one of the Waqifites who did not recognize Imam al-Riḍā (ʻa), once questioned him, "Can there be two Imams?"

Imam al-Riḍā (ʻa) replied, "No, except that one of them is silent."

The man then remarked, "But you do not have a silent one."

Imam al-Riḍāʾ (ʻa) said, "By Allah, He will grant me someone who will establish the truth and its people, and will destroy falsehood and its people." At that time, he had no children, but Abū Jaʿfar (ʻa) was born a year later.[3]

The Blessed Birth

It was the year 195 AH, in the month of Ramaḍān, when the loyal

---

1. *Biḥār al-Anwār,* vol. 50, p. 22.

2. Ibid.

3. Ibid.

Shīʿa were eagerly awaiting the birth of Imam al-Riḍā's son, as their traditions foretold of his coming as narrated by them from the Messenger (peace be upon him and his family) who said, "The best of handmaidens will choose the Nubians," referring to the Imam (peace be upon him), in order to refute the arguments of the Waqifites[1] who increased their claims against him.

It was the night of the 19th of the blessed month when the dawn of truth appeared, a full moon that became a guiding sun, a noble presence: Imam al-Jawād (peace be upon him). The narrators conveyed his father's words: "This is the child of whom there is no greater blessing born in Islam."[2]

Indeed, Imam al-Jawād (ʻa) was born at a time of great discord among the Shi'a. The propagandist claims of some opponents were reaching the hearts of some simple-minded followers. The birth of Imam al-Jawād (ʻa) affirmed Imam al-Riḍā's (ʻa) legitimacy and invalidated the claims of the Waqifiyya. As a result, the falsehoods of the Waqifiyya were washed away like salt in the ocean waves, and the birth of the Imam became a cause for the triumph of truth and the unification of the Shi'a, the followers of truth, after a period of discord. Furthermore, Imam al-Riḍā (ʻa) often said that his son would be his successor, though they did not see that he had a son. Even as he reached middle age, doubts arose among some of his naïve followers

1. The Waqifites, also known as the Waqifi Shia, were a sect within Shia Islam that emerged after the death of the seventh Imam, Musa al-Kadhim, in 799 CE. The term "Waqifites" comes from the Arabic word "waqf," meaning "stoppage" or "standing still," reflecting their belief that the line of Imamate stopped with Mūsā al-Kāẓim. The Waqifites held that Musa al-Kadhim did not die but went into occultation (*ghayba*). They rejected the Imamate of Ali al-Riḍā, the eighth Imam according to Ithnā ʿAsharī Shīʿa, and all subsequent Imams. They believed that recognizing any Imam after Mūsā al-Kāẓim was unnecessary and incorrect. However, over time, the Waqifite sect gradually diminished as most of its adherents either reverted to mainstream Ithnā ʿAsharī Shīʿa Islam or joined other sects.

2. *Biḥār al-Anwār,* vol. 50, p. 20.

until the birth of Imam al-Jawād (‘a) dispelled those doubts. The Shi'a rejoiced and praised Allah for the fulfillment of their prophecies.

Childhood

As a noble child, Imam al-Jawād (‘a) grew under the care of his great father just as a flower blossoms in the gentle breeze, receiving knowledge and manners from him. Thus, the noble lineage combined with the honor of ancestry, and the talents unfolded as the dawn unfolds into a radiant morning.

And by Allah's will, the child, even in his youth, became a master and an Imam.

He surpassed the entire era in his youth,	سبق الدهر كله في صباه
And time walked as a servant behind him.	و مشى الدهر خادماً من ورائه

When Imam al-Jawād (peace be upon him) was five years old, envoys from al-Ma'mūn, the Abbasid caliph, came to urge his father, Imam al-Riḍā (peace be upon him), to migrate to the new capital of the Islamic state, Khurāsān, and become the crown prince. This happened after Maʾmūn killed his brother Amīn. The circumstances forced Imam ʿAlī b. Mūsā (peace be upon him) to leave Medina for Khurāsān, the new capital of the Muslims. The war between the two Abbasid brothers, Amīn and Maʾmūn, had consumed much of the Muslims' energy, fueling the conflict. The revolution in Khurāsān was initially carried by the Shīʿa, who had supported the first Abbasid revolt against the Umayyad rule, only to have their revolution hijacked by deviant leaders, causing their efforts to go in vain. This second revolution was a strong reaction to the deviation of power inasmuch as it was taken away from the rightful family of the Prophet (s). Maʾmūn outwardly adopted Shiʿism and explicitly called for Shi'a principles at the beginning of his rule. He coerced Imam al-Riḍā (peace be upon him) to move to Khurāsān to reinforce the idea of his Shiʿism among his followers and then acted according to his own agenda.

Imam al-Riḍā (‘a) prepared to leave, fully aware of what awaited him after his departure. It was a journey with clear outlines, but it was a path the Imam had to follow according to the circumstances and the apparent teachings of Islam. He had to convey his message to fulfill his duty, spread true awareness among Muslims as much as possible, even if it cost him his precious life. He bid farewell to his family and appointed his son al-Jawād (‘a), who was only five years old, as their guardian, knowing well his gifted competence. Imam al-Riḍā (‘a) then traversed plains and mountains to Khurāsān, where he was welcomed by the faithful who made him their crown prince, set to inherit the Islamic caliphate after Maʾmūn. Correspondence between father and son continued, addressing both private and public matters.

Imam al-Riḍā (‘a) was greatly impressed by his son. When a letter came from al-Jawād (‘a) and he wanted to inform his followers, he would say, "Abū Jaʿfar wrote to me" or "I wrote to Abū Jaʿfar," never using "my son" nor his personal name, out of reverence and respect.

Meanwhile, in Medina, his pious son was visited by the Shi'a just as they visited his father al-Riḍā (peace be upon him), knowing that he was their future Imam, referred to as their "silent Imam."

One day, while the Shiʿa were in the presence of al-Jawād, peace be upon him, his demeanor changed, and he began to weep. When the servant arrived, he instructed him to prepare for mourning.

"Whose mourning? For whom do we mourn, may I be sacrificed for you?"

"The mourning for my father, Abul-Ḥassan al-Riḍā (peace be upon him). He was martyred at this very hour in Khurāsān."

"My father and mother be sacrificed for you, Khurāsān is thousands of miles away from Medina, separated by plains and mountains."

"Yes, a feeling from Allah Almighty came over me, one I had never known before. I knew then that my father had passed away."[1]

Imam al-Jawād (ʻa) was known by the *kunya* (teknonym) "Abū Jaʿfar" as a reminder of his grandfather Abū Jaʿfar Muḥammad al-Bāqir (peace be upon him), though he did not have a son named Jaʿfar. He was also given various titles such as al-Jawād, al-Taqī, al-Murtaḍā, al-Muntajab, and al-Qāniʿ. However, the most famous title was "Ibn al-Riḍā" (Son of al-Riḍā) because his father, Imam al-Riḍā, peace be upon him, had a widespread and excellent reputation among Muslims. Therefore, three of his sons were known by this title, including the ninth, tenth, and eleventh Imams, due to Imam al-Riḍā's well-known virtue and high standing among Muslims.

1. *Biḥār al-Anwār,* vol. 50, p. 63.

Chapter Two

His Life and Imamate

Imam al-Jawād (‘a) in Childhood

The concept of Imamate in the belief of the Shi'a who uphold it differs significantly from other interpretations. For the Shi'a, the term implies the absolute succession to the Prophet (s), encompassing his knowledge, wisdom, qualifications, and responsibilities. In other words, it represents a "complete image of prophethood," with the only distinction being that an Imam is not a recipient of divine revelation, whereas a Prophet is. Prophethood, in the context of Islam, is a unique capability bestowed by Allah upon a chosen individual, making him a mediator who receives divine revelation and disseminates it among his people. This idea, when applied to prophethood, similarly applies to Imamate with the same logic and proof. Just as it is conceivable that a child in the cradle could be a Prophet, it is equally conceivable for a child to be an Imam.

Although age is often a measure for people, it is not a measure with Allah. The elder is not always greater in the sight of Allah. An old man might be insignificant before his Lord, while a young person or child might be beloved by his Creator. Good deeds, pure intentions, and endowed capabilities are the primary measures in Islam and the logic of the Quran. Furthermore, belief in prophethood and Imamate necessitates complete faith in Allah's ability to endow an individual with all virtues, making him a source of knowledge and a model for people. Belief in prophethood implies belief in miracles, which transcend human capabilities, and distinguish the Prophet so he can lead and warn people on behalf of Allah.

A miracle, being something beyond the natural order, does not differentiate between an elder and a young individual, a wealthy person or a poor one. Historically, people often claimed that a prophet must be wealthy and noble among his people. Their prophets (peace be upon them) explained that if Allah wanted to bestow His mercy on an individual who did not meet these criteria and made him a prophet, what harm would there be? Allah says:

“Do they distribute the mercy of your Lord? We distribute among them their livelihood in the life of this world, and We have raised some of them above others in degrees that they may make use of one another for service. But the mercy of your Lord is better than what they accumulate.”[1]

Nations have often marveled and been amazed when Allah sent a young boy as a prophet. Allah made this deliberate to demonstrate the nature of prophethood: it is not a common gift bestowed on an individual by virtue of environment and upbringing but an extraordinary occurrence that transcends the natural order, proclaiming the unique ability of Allah and His ultimate power. ʿAlī b. Asbat narrates about Imamate: "I saw Abū Jaʿfar al-Jawād (peace be upon him) emerge before me, so I scrutinized him, from head to toe, to describe his stature to our companions in Egypt. He prostrated and said: 'Allah's argument in Imamate is the same as His argument in prophethood. Allah says:

“And We gave him judgment while yet a boy.”[2]

And Allah also said:

“And when he reached his full strength...”[3]

And He said:

“And when he reached forty years…”[4]

Thus, it is possible to be given wisdom as a boy or at forty years of

1. Quran, 43:32
2. Quran, 19:12
3. Quran, 12:22
4. Quran, 46:15

age.[1]

Indeed, if prophethood is a divine miracle and a sign of divine innovation, it matters not whether it manifests in old age or young age.

A narrator mentions being in the presence of Abū al-Ḥassan al-Riḍā (peace be upon him) in Khurāsān when someone asked: "My master, if something happens, to whom (does the Imamate pass)?" (meaning, if you die, who will be the Imam after you?).

He said: "To my son, Abū Jaʿfar."

The questioner seemed to doubt Abū Jaʿfar's young age. Abū al-Ḥassan (peace be upon him) said: "Allah sent Jesus as a prophet with a new divine law at an age younger than Abū Jaʿfar."

Indeed, there is no impossibility in what Allah wills and does. He made Jesus ('a) a prophet in his early childhood and granted Muḥammad b. ʿAlī ('a) the Imamate while still a child.

Imam Jaʿfar al-Ṣādiq ('a) had a son named ʿAlī b. Jaʿfar, who was highly respected by the Shīʿa. People would visit him to benefit from the knowledge he received directly from his father, al-Sadiq ('a), and his brother, Mūsā b. Jaʿfar ('a). One narrator recounts: "I was with ʿAlī b. Jaʿfar in Medina, where I had stayed for two years writing down what I heard from him, when Abū Jaʿfar Muḥammad b. ʿAlī b. Musa ('a) entered the mosque of the Messenger of Allah (peace be upon him and his family). ʿAlī b. Jaʿfar stood up without his cloak or shoes, kissed his hand, and honored him greatly. Abū Jaʿfar ('a) said: 'Uncle, sit down, may Allah have mercy on you.' ʿAlī b. Jaʿfar replied: 'My master, how can I sit while you are standing?' When ʿAlī b. Jaʿfar returned to his seat, his companions began to rebuke him, saying: 'You are his uncle, and yet you do this?' He replied: 'Be quiet! If Allah, the Exalted, has not seen fit to honor this old age of mine and has chosen this young man and placed him in the position He has, should I not acknowledge his virtue? We seek refuge in Allah from what you say;

1. *Biḥār al-Anwār,* vol. 50, p. 24-37.

rather, I am his servant.'"[1]

After His Father's Demise

Imam al-Riḍā (peace be upon him) passed away in Khurāsān, poisoned and buried in Tous (Ṭūs). His death caused turmoil within the Islamic community, which had flourished under his leadership. The caliphate returned to Baghdad, and Maʾmūn, who had previously taken the throne from his brother Amīn, altered his policies and betrayed those who supported him. He abandoned the half-Alawite slogan of the revolution and reverted to the black attire of the Abbasids, restoring the Abbasid state.

One day, Imam al-Jawād (ʻa) was walking through the crowded streets of Baghdad, where people lined up to catch a glimpse of the son of al-Riḍā (peace be upon him). Among them was a Zaydi man who recounted:

"I went to Baghdad and saw people jostling and standing in reverence. I asked what was happening and was told it was Ibn al-Riḍā (peace be upon him). I swore to see him for myself. He appeared, riding a mule. I cursed the followers of Imamate, questioning how they believed Allah had mandated obedience to such a person. He turned to me and said, 'O Qāsim b. ʿAbd al-Raḥmān: **"They said, "Shall we follow one of us who is but a human being? Indeed, we would then be in error and madness.'"**[2] I thought to myself, 'By Allah, he is a magician.' He then added: **'Was the message sent down upon him from among us? Rather, he is an insolent liar.'**[3] I left, convinced of the Imamate, testifying that he was Allah's proof to His creation, and I believed in him."[4]

The astonishment that filled this man's heart due to the Imam's young age was answered clearly through these two verses. Imam al-

1. Al-Kulaynī, *al-Kāfī,* vol.1, p. 322.

2. Quran, 54:24

3. Quran, 54:25

4. *Biḥār al-Anwār,* vol. 50, p. 64.

Jawād (peace be upon him), despite his youth, was highly regarded by Allah and people. The Shi'a, a significant community by then, had entrusted their affairs to him, and he managed them admirably. He gained the trust and following of many of his father's and grandfather's companions.

In Medina

Imam al-Jawād ('a) remained in Medina for about eight years after his father's demise. He was respected by everyone, receiving visitors from near and far who sought his guidance on various complex matters, which he resolved swiftly.

A narrator recalls: "After the demise of Abū al-Ḥassan al-Riḍā ('a), we performed Hajj and visited Abū Jaʿfar ('a). Shi'a from all regions came to see him. His uncle, ʿAbdullah b. Mūsā, a noble elderly man dressed in rough clothing with a prayer mark on his forehead, entered. Abū Jaʿfar ('a) emerged from his room wearing a fine shirt and robe and white sandals. His uncle stood up, greeted him with a kiss on his forehead, and the Shi'a followed suit. Abū Jaʿfar ('a) sat on a chair, and people, astonished by his youth, looked at each other in confusion.

A man from the group asked ʿAbdullah, 'May Allah preserve you. What is your ruling on a man who commits bestiality?'[1] ʿAbdullah replied, 'His hand should be cut off, and he should be punished.' Abū Jaʿfar ('a) angrily responded, 'Fear Allah, O uncle. You must be cautious in giving fatwas on the Day of Judgment before Allah. My father ('a) was asked about a man who desecrated a woman's grave and had intercourse with her. He said, "His hand is cut off for desecration, and he is lashed for fornication because the sanctity of the deceased is like the sanctity of the living." ʿAbdullah admitted his mistake, saying, 'You are right, my master. I seek forgiveness from Allah.' People were amazed and asked Abū Jaʿfar ('a) if they could

1. Sexual intercourse between a person and an animal.

ask him questions. He consented, and they asked him about thirty thousand issues, all of which he answered at the age of nine."[1]

This story highlights the significance of the Imam in the eyes of the Shi'a, the extent of his knowledge, and the breadth of his culture, which stemmed from a heart filled with Allah's knowledge, piety, and fear.

To Baghdad

When Maʾmūn, the Abbasid King, moved to Baghdad, he was in constant conflict with the Abbasids, who condemned his appointment of al-Riḍā (ʻa) as his successor. They reminded him that the descendants of Fāṭima (ʻa) were the most feared adversaries, having supporters and loyalists in both the eastern and western parts of the country.

Maʾmūn justified his position about ʿAlī b. Musa (ʻa) by extolling his virtues, which even Maʾmūn and others struggled to enumerate fully. He said that the members of this household had inherited knowledge from their ancestors, just as they had inherited noble qualities and high moral standards.

At that time, the Shīʿa had strengthened their position through Imam al-Riḍā (ʻa), gaining devoted advocates in every corner of the Islamic lands. The general public leaned towards them due to the manifest virtues and perfection displayed by Imam al-Riḍā, peace be

1. Ibid., p. 85. It is possible that he was only eight years old, as mentioned in some narrations. What appears from this narration is that the Shīʿa had gathered in Medina during the season right after the death of Imam al-Ridha. Imam al-Jawād (peace be upon him) was seven years old when he passed away at the end of the month of Safar. After seven months, the month of Ramaḍān came, and al-Jawād entered his eighth year. In the Hajj season of that year, this dialogue took place. It is also possible that the questions were directed to the Imam over several days within the same session, making his session resemble conferences that last for consecutive days, spent in discussions except for times of rest and meals.

upon him, in the political arena.

The call for the Imamate of the descendants of Fatima (ʻa) spread more than ever before, as many of them held high positions in the state and were actively involved due to the conflict among the Abbasids. The authorities realized that many factions within the Abbasids themselves were plotting against the state, seeking power for themselves, which forced them to employ the Shīʿa as opponents to these factions.

On the other hand, there was a wave of public discontent due to Maʾmūn's killing of al-Riḍā (ʻa). To cover his betrayal of al-Riḍā (ʻa) and to placate the general public, as well as to appease the non-Abbasid elite, Maʾmūn sent an official invitation to Imam al-Jawād (ʻa) in Medina.

This occurred in the year 211 AH, when Abū Jaʿfar al-Jawād (ʻa) was about sixteen years old. Historical accounts suggest that the reception of the Imam was marked by royal celebrations prepared by the caliph for his blessed guest. The people eagerly anticipated the arrival of Imam al-Riḍā's son, longing to see and be in his presence.

Maʾmūn received him with great honor and intended to marry him to his daughter, Umm al-Faḍl, just as he had married his own daughter, Umm Ḥabīb, to Imam al-Riḍā (ʻa). However, the Abbasids strongly objected, fearing that the caliphate might pass to the descendants of Fāṭima (ʻa).

They gathered his close relatives and said to him, "We implore you by Allah, O Commander of the Faithful, not to proceed with this decision you have made to marry your daughter to al-Riḍā's son. We fear that through him we will lose the power that Allah Almighty has granted us, and the honor He has bestowed upon us will be taken away. You know well the longstanding enmity between us and these people. We were already anxious about your actions concerning al-Riḍā (ʻa), but Allah spared us from harm in that matter. We beseech you not to return us to a distress from which we have been relieved."

Maʾmūn replied to them, "The discord between you and the family of Abū Ṭālib is your own doing. If you had been just to them, it would have been better for you. As for what my predecessors did to them, it was an act of severing kinship, and I seek refuge in Allah from that. I do not regret appointing al-Riḍā (ʻa) as my successor. I asked him to take up the leadership, and I would step down, but he refused. Allah's command was a destined decree.

As for Abū Jaʿfar Muḥammad b. ʿAlī (i.e. Imam al-Jawād), I have chosen him because he surpasses all others in knowledge and culture, despite his young age. I hope that what I have recognized in him will become evident to the people, so you will know that my judgment about him is correct."

They said, "Although this young man has impressed you with his demeanor, he is a boy with no knowledge or understanding. Allow him time to mature, then you can proceed as you see fit."

Maʾmūn replied, "Woe to you! I know this young man better than you do. The knowledge of this household is from Allah Almighty. His ancestors have always been rich in religious knowledge and etiquette, needless of the people who do not have knowledge of anything. If you wish, you can test Abū Jaʿfar (ʻa) with something that will prove his knowledge to you."

They agreed to this and asked to question him in the presence of Maʾmūn on matters of Islamic jurisprudence. If he answered correctly, they would have no objection, and it would become clear to the public that the opinion of the Commander of the Faithful was sound. If he failed, they would be spared from his matter. Maʾmūn agreed, and they decided that Yaḥyā b. Aktham, the chief judge of the Islamic territories at that time, would question Imam al-Jawād (ʻa) on obscure issues of Islamic jurisprudence.

The appointed time came, and the people gathered. Imam al-Jawād (ʻa) arrived, and Yaḥyā b. Aktham was present. Yaḥyā sat in front of him, and Maʾmūn sat beside the Imam, overseeing the assembly. Yaḥyā turned to the caliph and asked, "Do you permit me, O Commander of the Faithful, to ask Abū Jaʿfar a question?" Maʾmūn told him to seek the Imam's permission. Yaḥyā turned to the Imam and said, "May I be your ransom, do you permit me to ask a question?" Abū Ja'far ('a) replied, "Ask whatever you wish."

Yaḥyā asked, "What do you say, may I be your ransom, about a pilgrim in the state of iḥrām who kills a prey?"

Abū Ja'far asked: "Did he kill it within the sanctuary or outside? Was he knowledgeable about the prohibition or ignorant? Did he kill it intentionally or by mistake? Was he free or a slave? Was he a minor or an adult? Was this his first time killing or had he done it before? Was the prey a bird or something else? Was it a small prey or a large one? Was he persistent in what he did or regretful? Did he kill it during the night or the day? Was he in the state of iḥrām for 'umrah when he killed it or for ḥajj?"[1]

Yaḥyā b. Aktham was bewildered and it showed on his face. He stammered until the audience realized his predicament. Ma'mūn then said, "Praise be to Allah for this blessing and for guiding me in my opinion." He turned to his relatives and said, "Do you now understand what you were denying?" Then he turned to Abū Ja'far ('a) and said, "Do you wish to propose, O Abū Ja'far?" The Imam replied, "Yes, O Commander of the Faithful." Ma'mūn said, "Propose for yourself, may I be your ransom, for I have accepted you for myself and I will marry you to my daughter Umm al-Faḍl, even if some people dislike

1. In these following paragraphs, his scholarly prowess becomes evident, demonstrating his remarkable ability to dissect questions. It has long been said that breaking down the question is half the answer. In addition to his quick wit and exceptional intelligence, he thoroughly understands all aspects of the issue. Each binary question posed by the Imam (peace be upon him) addresses the preceding question and anticipates the subsequent one.

   This method of questioning works as follows: If the killing occurred outside the sanctuary, it falls into two categories—either the pilgrim was knowledgeable or ignorant. Similarly, if the killing occurred within the sanctuary, it too divides into two categories—either the pilgrim was knowledgeable or ignorant, and so on.

it."

Abū Jaʿfar (ʻa) said, "Praise be to Allah in acknowledgment of His blessings, and there is no Allah but Allah, the One. May Allah bless Muḥammad, the leader of His creation, and the chosen ones from his progeny. As for what follows, it is by the grace of Allah upon the people that He has made them free from forbidden things by lawful means. Allah Almighty said, **"And marry those among you who are single and the righteous among your male slaves and female slaves. If they are poor, Allah will enrich them from His bounty. And Allah is All-Encompassing, All-Knowing."**[1]

Then, Muḥammad b. ʿAlī b. Mūsā seeks the hand of Umm al-Faḍl, daughter of Abdullah al-Maʾmūn. He has offered her the dowry of his grandmother Fāṭima, daughter of Muḥammad (peace be upon him and his family), which is five hundred dirhams in gold coins. O Commander of the Faithful, have you married her to him on this dowry?"

Maʾmūn replied, "Yes, I have married her to you, O Abū Jaʿfar, on the mentioned dowry. Do you accept the marriage?" Abū Jaʿfar (ʻa) said, "I accept and am pleased with it."

The Wedding Ceremony

The narrator said: "We soon heard sounds resembling those of sailors in conversation, when the servants came pulling a boat made of surplus materials, tied with silk ropes, on a wheel filled with perfume (a type of fragrance). Maʾmūn ordered that the bark of the elite be perfumed with that fragrance, and then it was extended to the common people so they could also enjoy the scent. Tables were set, and people ate, and gifts were distributed to each group according to their status. When the crowd dispersed and only a few of the elite remained, Maʾmūn said to Abū Jaʿfar (ʻa): 'If you don't mind, may I

1. Sūrah al-Nūr, 24:32

request that we discuss the jurisprudence regarding the killing of game (prey)?'

Abū Jaʿfar (ʻa) responded: 'Yes. If a pilgrim kills game in the sanctuary and the game is a bird and of large size, he must sacrifice a sheep. If he kills it in the sacred precinct, he must double the penalty. If he kills a chick in the sanctuary, he must offer a suckling lamb. If he kills it in the sacred precinct, he must offer the lamb and the value of the chick. If it is a wild animal and he kills a wild donkey, he must sacrifice a cow. If it is an ostrich, he must sacrifice a camel. If it is a gazelle, he must sacrifice a sheep. If he kills any of these in the sacred precinct, he must double the penalty and offer it as a sacrifice to the Kaʿba. If the pilgrim is obligated to offer a sacrifice and his pilgrimage is for Hajj, he must sacrifice it at Mina. If his pilgrimage is for Umrah, he must sacrifice it in Mecca. The penalty for killing game is the same for the knowledgeable and the ignorant. Deliberate action incurs a sin, but it is forgiven for mistakes. The expiation is upon the free person for himself, and upon the master for his slave. A minor has no expiation, but an adult must pay it. Repentance absolves the penitent from the punishment in the afterlife, but persistence in the sin requires punishment in the afterlife.'

Maʾmūn said: 'Well said, Abū Jaʿfar (ʻa), may Allah reward you. If you don't mind, would you ask Yaḥyā a question as he asked you?'

Abū Jaʿfar (ʻa) asked Yaḥyā: 'Shall I ask you a question?"

Yaḥyā replied: "It is up to you—may I be your sacrifice—if I know the answer, I will reply, and if not, I will learn from you.'

Abū Jaʿfar (ʻa) asked: 'Tell me about a man who looked at a woman in the morning, and it was forbidden for him to look at her. By mid-morning, she became permissible for him. At noon, she became forbidden to him again. In the afternoon, she became permissible for him. At sunset, she became forbidden again. At the time of the evening prayer, she became permissible. At midnight, she became forbidden again. At dawn, she became permissible. What is the status of this woman, and how did she become permissible and forbidden to him?'

Yaḥyā replied: 'By Allah, I do not know the answer to this question, nor do I understand its reasoning. Please enlighten us.'

Abū Jaʿfar ('a) said: 'This woman is a slave girl of a man. An outsider looked at her in the morning, which was forbidden for him. By mid-morning, he bought her from her master, so she became permissible for him. At noon, he freed her, so she became forbidden to him. In the afternoon, he married her, so she became permissible for him. At sunset, he declared her unlawful by comparing her to his mother (a form of oath in Islamic law), so she became forbidden. At the time of the evening prayer, he atoned for his oath, so she became permissible. At midnight, he divorced her once, so she became forbidden. At dawn, he took her back, so she became permissible.'

Maʾmūn turned to those present from his family and asked: "Is there anyone among you who can answer this question in the same way or understands the previous question?'

They replied: 'By Allah, no, the Commander of the Faithful is more knowledgeable and discerning.'

Maʾmūn said: 'Woe unto you! The members of this house[1] are distinguished by the virtues you see, and their youth does not prevent them from attaining perfection. Do you not know that the Messenger of Allah (peace be upon him and his family) began his mission by inviting ʿAlī b. Abī Ṭālib ('a) when he was ten years old, accepted his Islam, and judged him by it, without calling anyone else (to Islam) of his age? He took the allegiance of al-Ḥassan and al-Ḥusayn (peace be upon them) when they were less than six years old and did not take the allegiance of any other child besides them. Do you not know what Allah has exclusively bestowed upon these people? They are descendants one from another, and the later ones follow the same path as the earlier ones.'

They said: 'You are right, O Commander of the Faithful.' Then the

1. The Household of the Holy Prophet, piece be upon him and his family.

group dispersed.

The Prizes and Gifts

The next day, people gathered, including Abū Jaʿfar (ʿa), and the commanders, courtiers, elites, and officials came to congratulate Maʾmūn and Abū Jaʿfar (ʿa). Three silver trays were brought out, containing musk-saffron balls.[1] Inside these balls were slips of paper with written notes of substantial sums of money, valuable gifts, and grants in the form of pieces of land.[2] Maʾmūn ordered these to be scattered among his special entourage. Whoever picked up one of these balls would open the slip inside and present it to Maʾmūn, who would then grant them the specified gift.

The trays were emptied, scattering their contents among the commanders and other high-ranking officials. People left enriched with gifts and rewards. Maʾmūn also ordered charity to be given to all the poor. He continued to honor Abū Jaʿfar (ʿa) and held him in high esteem throughout his life, favoring him over his own children and other family members.[3]

When the marriage of the Imam to Maʾmūn's daughter was completed, the Imam stayed in Baghdad for a considerable period, enjoying a life of ease. Muslims would visit him, drawing from his wisdom and benefiting from his guidance, which enriched and fulfilled them. However, he was not content with living luxuriously in the Abbasid palaces, neglecting the religious affairs of the Shīʿa and Muslims. It seems that if circumstances had not compelled him to stay in Baghdad, he would not have remained there for long.

One of his companions narrates: "I visited him in Baghdad and

---

1. A round thing resembling a walnut.
2. Kings used to grant some individuals large plots of princely lands, and they were called iqtāʿ (lit. plots).
3. *Al-Iḥtijāj*, pp. 227-229; *Biḥār al-anwār*, vol. 50, pp. 73-77.

reflected on the blessings he enjoyed. I thought to myself, 'This man will never return to his homeland.' He then lowered his head and, after a moment, raised it with a pale face, saying: 'O Husayn, barley bread and coarse salt in the vicinity of the Messenger of Allah are dearer to me than what you see.'"[1]

Back to Medina

He traveled to Medina via Kūfa. Upon his arrival in Kūfa, the Shīʿa gathered to welcome him with great enthusiasm. He then bid them farewell and continued to his grandfather's city, where he spent the rest of his life fulfilling his significant responsibilities, including establishing a comprehensive intellectual school, until the death of Maʾmūn.

After Maʾmūn

Maʾmūn made a will to his brother Muʿtaṣim before passing away in a village near Ṭarsūs, which was a border area between the Islamic lands and the Roman territories, where clashes had erupted. The Caliph himself had gone there until the Muslims achieved victory. He specifically instructed Muʿtaṣim regarding the Alawites, saying: "These are your cousins, the descendants of the Commander of the Faithful, ʿAlī (ʿa). Treat them well, overlook their faults, and maintain their stipends annually, as their rights are numerous."

In late summer, on the night of the 12th of Rajab in the year 218 AH, Maʾmūn passed away and was buried in the outskirts of Ṭarsūs. Muʿtaṣim then took the reins of power, striving to consolidate his rule by all means. He considered Imam al-Jawād (ʿa), who was the son-in-law of the late Caliph and the leader of the Shīʿa—a formidable force within the nation—a potential threat to the state. Therefore, he summoned him from Medina to Baghdad, not for any specific reason

1. *Mukhtār al-Kharāʾij wa al-Jarāʾiḥ,* p. 208.

other than to keep the Imam under his personal surveillance. The Imam moved to Baghdad for the second time, distancing himself from the royal court and engaging in public affairs. This period lasted from the 28th of Muḥarram in the year 220 AH until the 29th of Dhūl-Qaʿdah of the same year, when he passed away due to poison administered by the authorities, under the directive of Caliph al-Muʿtaṣim. This story is narrated by the esteemed author al-ʿAyāshī, through the account of the servant and confidant of Ibn Abī Dāwūd, known as Wanān. Ibn Abī Dāwūd was a famous judge in Baghdad. He said:

Ibn Abī Dawud returned one day upon visiting Muʿtaṣim presence feeling troubled. I asked him why, and he said: "Because of what happened today with this black man," referring to Abū Jaʿfar al-Jawād (ʻa), "in the presence of the Commander of the Faithful."

I asked, "What happened?"

He said: "A thief had confessed to his theft and requested the Caliph to purify him through punishment. The jurists were gathered, and Muḥammad b. ʿAlī (ʻa) was also brought in. We were asked about the limit and extent of the hand amputation for theft. I said it should be at the wrist joint (the joint between the hand and the arm). He asked for the evidence, and I cited the verse in the Quran regarding ablution: **'Then perform tayammum with clean earth and rub with it your faces and hands.'**[1] A group agreed with me, while others said the cut should be at the elbow because Allah says regarding ablution: **'And your hands up to the elbows'**, indicating that the hand extends to the elbow.

Muʿtaṣim then turned to Muḥammad b. ʿAlī (ʻa) and asked: "What do you say, Abū Jaʿfar (ʻa)?" He replied: "The scholars have already spoken on this matter, O Commander of the Faithful." Al-Muʿtaṣim insisted: "Leave aside what they have said. What do you have to say?" Abū Jaʿfar (ʻa) said: "Excuse me for this, O Commander of the Faithful." Muʿtaṣim said: "I adjure you by Allah to tell us what you

1. Quran 5:6

have." He said: "If you adjure me by Allah, then I say that they have erred in this matter. The amputation should be at the joint of the fingers, leaving the palm intact." Muʿtaṣim asked: "What is your evidence for this?"

He replied: "The saying of the Messenger of Allah (peace be upon him and his family): 'Prostration is to be done on seven body parts: the face, the hands, the knees, and the feet.' If the hand is cut off at the wrist or elbow, the person would no longer have a hand to prostrate on, while Allah, the Exalted, has said: **'And the places of prostration are for Allah**[1], referring to these seven body parts that one prostrates on. What is for Allah should not be cut off."

Muʿtaṣim was impressed by this and ordered that the thief's hand be cut off at the joint of the fingers, leaving the palm intact.

Ibn Abī Dawud continued, "My world turned upside down, and I wished I had never been alive. Three days later, I went to Muʿtaṣim and said: 'It is my duty to advise the Commander of the Faithful, and I will speak of something that I know may send me to hell.' Muʿtaṣim asked: 'What is it?' I replied: 'When the Commander of the Faithful gathers the jurists of his realm and the scholars for a matter of religious concern and asks them about the ruling, they provide their opinions in the presence of his commanders, ministers, and scribes. The people outside hear about this, yet he discards all their opinions for the ruling of one man, a man whom half of this nation considers their Imam and claims that he has more right to the Caliphate than the Commander of the Faithful himself. Then he rules according to this man's opinion, disregarding the jurists' views!' Muʿtaṣim's color changed, realizing the point I had made. He said: 'May Allah reward you for your advice.'

On the fourth day, Muʿtaṣim ordered someone (the name was omitted by some writers or narrators) among his ministers to invite Imam al-Jawād (ʿa) to his home. The minister invited him, but the Imam refused, saying: 'You know I do not attend your gatherings.' The

1. Quran 72:18

minister insisted: 'I am only inviting you for a meal. I wish for you to honor my home and bless it with your presence.' Imam al-Jawād (ʻa) finally agreed. (The minister poisoned the food.) After eating, the Imam felt the poison. He called for his mount and, as he was leaving, the host asked him to stay longer. Al-Jawad (ʻa) replied: 'Leaving your home is better for you.' He spent that day and night struggling with the poison spreading through his body until he passed away.

Alas! The Imam of truth! Is this your reward after all the good you did for them? They sought nothing but evil for you. Cursed are they, and blessed are you. They deceived and plotted against you by poisoning you in the prime of your youth. But you have a noble example in your forefathers, while they have a disgraceful lineage. Peace be upon you, and curses be upon them.

Indeed, that brilliant light was extinguished, leaving the Islamic nation to grieve deeply, like the earth mourns after the setting of the sun. Imam al-Jawād (ʻa) was the youngest of the Twelve Imams, except for Imam al-Mahdi (ʻa), when he inherited the spiritual leadership in the end of Safar in the year 202 AH, at the age of seven.

Imam al-Jawād (ʻa) was also the youngest among them at the time of his martyrdom at the age of twenty-five, having held the Imamate for eighteen years. The entire city of Baghdad was in mourning upon the death of Ibn al-Riḍā (ʻa). Suspicions arose about the palace, and there was almost an uprising against the unjust rule. He was prayed over by both the son of Muʿtaṣim, al-Wāthiq Billāh, and his noble son, Imam ʿAlī al-Hadi (ʻa). He was buried in his resting place in Kāẓimiyya, where he continues to be visited and honored. Peace and blessings be upon Muḥammad b. ʿAlī al-Jawād (ʻa).

In some accounts, it is said that Muʿtaṣim called some of his ministers and ordered them to testify against Muḥammad b. ʿAlī al-Jawād (ʻa), accusing him of intending to incite a revolt with his followers from the Shīʿa Imamiyya. This was to make it easier for Muʿtaṣim to imprison or kill him. When the Imam was brought before him, Muʿtaṣim said: "You intended to rebel against me." The Imam replied: "By Allah, I have done nothing of the sort." Muʿtaṣim said: "So-and-so and so-and-so have testified against you." They were brought forth, and they said: "Yes, these are the letters we took from some of your servants." The Imam, who was seated in a hall, raised his hand and said: "O Allah, if they have lied about me, then take them." The narrator said: "We saw the hall shaking, and they would get up only to fall again."

Muʿtaṣim said: "O son of the Messenger of Allah (s), I repent for what I have done. Pray to your Lord to calm it." The Imam said: "O Allah, calm it, for You know that they are Your enemies and mine." And it calmed down.[1]

Al-Jawād's (ʻa) presence in Baghdad after marrying Muʿtaṣim's daughter was filled with much respect and honor, yet he longed to return to his homeland. He often expressed that a simple life near the Prophet's sanctuary was dearer to him than the luxury in Baghdad. Eventually, he returned to Medina, only to be summoned again to Baghdad under the pretext of being a threat to the state. It was during this second stay in Baghdad, from the 28th of Muharram 220 AH to the 29th of Dhūl-Qaʿdah 220 AH, that he was poisoned on the orders of Muʿtaṣim. Imam al-Jawād (peace be upon him) died a martyr in his prime, leaving behind a legacy of wisdom, piety, and unparalleled knowledge.

May Allah's peace and blessings be upon Muḥammad b. ʿAlī al-Jawād (peace be upon him), and may His wrath and punishment be upon those who wronged him.

1. *Mukhtār al-Kharāʾij wa al-Jarāʾiḥ,* p. 237.

Chapter Three

The Imam and His Era

The Imam's Era[1]

Imam Muḥammad b. ʿAlī al-Jawād (ʻa) lived through the reigns of two Abbasid caliphs. The caliph during whose rule the Imam experienced relatively calm conditions was al-Maʾmūn al-ʿAbbāsī. It is well known that Maʾmūn sought to align himself with the Alawites and their leader, Imam ʿAlī b. Mūsā al-Riḍā (ʻa), due to the public pressure on the Abbasid regime, which faced a series of revolts and uprisings across the Islamic state.

Some historians suggest that Maʾmūn was a Shi'ite and believed in the rightful claim of Imam ʿAlī's (ʻa) descendants to the caliphate and the Imamate of Imam ʿAlī (ʻa). However, this perspective on Maʾmūn is not accepted because such an honor is not deserved by an usurping caliph.

It is important to note that after the martyrdom of Imam al-Riḍā (ʻa) at the hands of Maʾmūn, Muḥammad b. ʿAlī al-Jawād (ʻa) became the legitimate Imam for the followers of the prophetic mission. It is also known that Imam al-Jawād (ʻa) became a son-in-law of Maʾmūn, the Abbasid king.

Why did the Imam marry the caliph's daughter? To understand why Imam al-Jawād (ʻa) married Maʾmūn's daughter, we need to look at the missionary movement led and expanded by the Imams (ʻa) during the times of Imam al-Riḍā (ʻa) and his son Imam al-Jawād (ʻa).

Under Maʾmūn's rule, the missionary movement evolved into one

---

1. This chapter was excerpted from *Islamic History* by the same author, p.343, and p. 348 and 355.

that could interact with the system and benefit from its protection, or even form what is today called a coalition government with any state. The Imams (ʻa) accepted protection from the state without compromising their mission.

The infallible Imams (ʻa) did not dissolve their movement, meaning they did not accept the caliphate nor participated in it. Evidence of this is Imam al-Riḍā's acceptance of the position of crown prince on the condition of non-interference in state affairs.

When Imam al-Jawād (ʻa) proposed to and married Maʾmūn's daughter, he became the caliph's son-in-law and used this position for his mission. What does it mean for someone to become the caliph's son-in-law?

Those who enter the court can become governors of a region, rulers of a country, or at least chief judges. However, Imam al-Jawād (ʻa) did none of these things. Instead, he took his wife and went to Medina, staying there until Maʾmūn's death.

What did the Imam gain from this marriage? Imam al-Jawād (ʻa) gained two things from this action:

1. He prevented Maʾmūn from assassinating him by accepting the marriage to his daughter.

2. He contained the claws and fangs of the authority within the confines of the missionary movement, as Maʾmūn could no longer dare to harm the movement's leaders and members.

This approach was often employed during the eras of various Imams (ʻa). A notable example is the story of ʿAlī b. Yaqṭīn b. Mūsā al-Baghdādī, who was an advisor to Caliph al-Mahdī al-ʿAbbāsī and later became a minister for Hārūn al-Rashīd. When he attained this position, maintaining a missionary direction, he approached Imam al-Ṣādiq (ʻa) and said, "O son of the Messenger of Allah, I have become an aide to this tyrant," and wished to resign. It is known that someone holding such a position at that time would control the largest state in the world.

The Imam asked him to remain in his role and continue performing his missionary duties while staying in Hārūn's court. He repeatedly asked the Imam for permission to leave the authority, but the Imam did not allow it. His contributions to the movement were significant, so much so that Imam Abū al-Ḥassan ('a) said of him when Dāwūd al-Raqī visited him on the day of sacrifice: "No one entered my heart while I was at the place (Minā') except 'Alī b. Yaqṭīn, for he was always with me and never left me until I finished."[1]

The Era of al-Mu'taṣim al-'Abbāsī

Imam al-Jawād ('a) lived during the reign of a caliph who had a direct impact on the downfall of the Abbasid state, al-Mu'taṣim al-'Abbāsī. Al-Mu'taṣim was the son of a Turkish concubine and showed a preference for his maternal relatives. He had a penchant for gathering Turks, purchasing them from their masters, and eventually amassed four thousand of them. He dressed them in various kinds of luxurious silks and golden accessories, distinguishing them from the rest of the soldiers.[2]

He assigned them leadership positions in the army, which led to unrest among the Arab soldiers. For instance, 'Ujayf tried to overthrow al-Mu'taṣim and place 'Abbas b. Ma'mūn on the throne, but the attempt failed, and al-Mu'taṣim had him killed.

The Turks, upon their arrival in the Islamic lands, gradually began to dominate the government, stripping the caliphs of their real power and initiating what we would now call military coups. They reached a point where if an Abbasid caliph diverged from their interests, they would assassinate him and install another member of the Abbasid house in his place. From al-Mutawakkil to al-Musta'īn, al-Muhtadī, and ending with al-Muqtadir, all these caliphs were killed by Turkish military leaders.

1. 'Allāma Ardabīlī, *Jāmi' al-Ruwāt,* vol. 1, p. 609.

2. Al-Mas'ūdī, vol. 3, p. 465.

Thus, they would depose and kill any caliph whose desires did not align with theirs, not because of anything inherent in the Turkish ethnicity, but due to the deteriorated state of the Islamic society, characterized by widespread moral decay and corruption.

Imam al-Jawād (‘a) took advantage of this situation to nurture the missionary movements that were preparing for the future. During this period, the revolution led by Muḥammad b. al-Qāsim b. ʿAlī al-Ṭālibī troubled the authorities, preventing them from living in peace and tranquility.

An Example of the Alawite Uprising

The revolt of Muḥammad b. al-Qāsim b. ʿAlī b. ʿUmar, son of Imam Zayn al-ʿĀbidīn ʿAlī b. al-Ḥusayn (‘a), was the most notable uprising during the era of Imam al-Jawād (‘a). Muḥammad b. al-Qāsim was highly esteemed, as evident from the chronicles of his *jihād*. The public nicknamed him "the Sufi" because he habitually wore coarse white woolen garments. He was known for his knowledge, piety, and asceticism.

He traveled to Merv in the province of Khurāsān, accompanied by a few men from Kūfa, after leaving Kūfa. Before that, he had gone to the vicinity of Raqqa with a group of prominent Zaydī figures, including Yaḥyā b. al-Ḥassan b. al-Furāt and ʿAbbād b. Yaʿqūb al-Rawajanī. The Zaydī’s often formed the backbone of numerous revolts.

Ibrāhīm b. Abdul-ʿAṭṭār narrated: "We were with him, and we dispersed among the people to invite them to his cause. It was not long before forty thousand responded and pledged allegiance to him. We settled him in one of the districts of Merv, where all the inhabitants were Shīʿa. They housed him in a fortress that even birds could not reach, atop a fortified mountain."[1]

1. Ibid.

Once, he heard crying in Merv and sent one of his companions to investigate. The companion returned with news that one of those people who had paid allegiance to him had wrongfully seized something from another man. Muḥammad reconciled them and then said to his companion Ibrāhīm: "O Ibrāhīm, can Allah's religion be supported by such means? Then he said: Disperse the people from me until I can decide."

He chose the righteous from among those who pledged allegiance to him and proceeded with them. This is an example of the nature of the missionary revolts; they did not permit any means to justify the ends. Just as the goal was to establish the rule of Allah Almighty, the means had to be pleasing to Allah as well.

This approach cultivated a society that cherished lofty ideals and noble principles. After purifying his companions, they set out for Ṭāliqān.

Ibrāhīm's Account of the Alawite Revolt

Ibrāhīm, Muḥammad b. al-Qāsim's companion, narrates:

"Muḥammad b. al-Qāsim immediately set out for Ṭāliqān, which was forty parasangs from Merv. He settled there, and we dispersed to invite people to his cause. Soon, a large number gathered around him. We approached him and said, 'If you complete your mission and confront the regime, we hope Allah will grant you victory. Once you succeed, you can then choose from your soldiers those whom you deem fit. However, if you act as you did in Merv, selecting only the righteous, ʿAbdullah b. Ṭāhir will track you down.' Ibrāhīm, his companion, tried to dissuade him from excluding those who were not strictly committed from the revolutionary army."

But Muḥammad b. al-Qāsim refused this advice. He engaged in numerous battles with ʿAbdullah b. Ṭāhir, inflicting severe defeats upon him.

Once, a temporary lull occurred in their conflicts, prompting

ʿAbdullah b. Ṭāhir to craft a cunning plan. He divided his army into units and told his chief commander, Ibrāhīm b. Ghassān b. Faraj al-ʿAwdī:

"I have assigned you a thousand elite horsemen and instructed them to carry a hundred thousand dirhams for any necessary expenses. Take three fine horses from my stable for your use and have a guide I have designated to accompany you. Give the guide a thousand dirhams and one of the horses to ride ahead. When you are one parasang from Nisā (where Muḥammad b. al-Qāsim was), open my letter, read it, and follow its instructions precisely. Be aware that I have an informant among your companions who will report every detail to me. Be very cautious."

This shows ʿAbdullah b. Ṭāhir's fear that his commander might sympathize with Muḥammad b. al-Qāsim. Such concerns were natural as the public supported the revolutionary movement, but the authorities used various tactics to suppress it, including threats, enticements, corruption, and surveillance. Ibn Ṭāhir stated, "I have spies watching your every breath."

The commander reached Nisā and, a parasang away, opened Ibn Ṭāhir's letter. The letter contained detailed plans, the location of Muḥammad b. al-Qāsim's residence, and his companion Abū Turāb. It instructed him to arrest them with heavy chains, send Ibn Ṭāhir his seal along with Muḥammad's seal as soon as they were captured, and to inform him immediately.

The plan succeeded, and Muḥammad b. al-Qāsim and Abū Turāb were taken to Ibn Ṭāhir in Nīshābūr. When Ibn Ṭāhir saw them, he rebuked his commander:

"Woe to you, Ibrāhīm! Did you not fear Allah in your actions?" referring to the extremely heavy chains placed on Muḥammad and his companion.

The commander replied:

"Commander, my fear of you made me forget my fear of Allah, and your promises made me oblivious to everything else."

They spoke from a balcony overlooking the room where Muḥammad b. al-Qāsim was imprisoned. Ibn Ṭāhir ordered the heavy chains to be replaced with lighter ones, allowing some mobility, and during his imprisonment, Muḥammad requested a copy of the Quran to study.

Abdullah b. Tahir then employed a deceptive tactic to transport Muḥammad secretly from Nīshābūr to Rey. He used mules with canopies to give the impression that Muḥammad was being transported openly while secretly moving him at night. This ruse continued until they reached Baghdad, where they presented him to al-Muʿtaṣim.

Upon hearing of Muḥammad's arrival, al-Muʿtaṣim ordered that his turban be removed, his head uncovered, and the canopy removed from his mule to humiliate him. The streets of Baghdad were crowded with people as Muḥammad was brought in. He was then taken to al-Muʿtaṣim's court, where he was mocked and humiliated in a setting of revelry and drink.

It is said that al-Muʿtaṣim's guards hurled filth at the gathered public while al-Muʿtaṣim laughed, and Muḥammad b. al-Qāsim continued to praise Allah, seeking forgiveness and praying against them. Al-Muʿtaṣim eventually ordered his imprisonment.

Muḥammad b. al-Qāsim soon devised a clever escape plan, disappearing from sight in Baghdad and then to Wāsiṭ, where he tightened his belt to support his weakened back from the ordeal. He remained hidden until the end of al-Muʿtaṣim and Muḥammad al-Wāthiq's reigns, and into part of al-Mutawakkil's reign. It is said he was eventually captured, imprisoned, and died in captivity.

What did he do during his time in hiding? This period, which was not short, saw Muḥammad b. al-Qāsim remaining hidden, but his influence persisted. The numerous revolts during the reign of al-Mutawakkil, al-Mustaʿīn, and subsequent caliphs continuously troubled the caliphate, preventing any peace or leisure for the rulers.

In Wāsiṭ, Muḥammad resided in the house of the mother of his cousin, ʿAlī b. al-Ḥassan b. ʿAlī b. ʿUmar, son of Imam Zayn al-Ābidīn (ʻa). This woman was an old and incapacitated lady. When she saw Muḥammad, she jumped up in joy, exclaiming: "Muḥammad, by Allah! May my life and family be sacrificed for you. Praise be to Allah for your safety!" She stood on her feet, which she had not done for years.

Ibrāhīm al-ʿAwdī, the commander of Ibn Ṭāhir's armies, described Muḥammad as follows:

"I have never seen anyone more dedicated, more chaste, or more frequently engaged in the remembrance of Allah, with such a strong spirit. He faced his ordeals without showing distress, brokenness, or submission. He was never seen joking, laughing, or making light-hearted comments except once. That was when they descended from the Halwan pass, and he was about to mount. One of Ibrāhīm b. Ghassān al-ʿAwdī's men stooped to allow him to mount the mule. When he was settled on the saddle, he said jokingly to the man: 'Do you take the stipends of the Abbasids and serve the sons of ʿAlī b. Abī Ṭālib?' and he smiled."

They offered Muḥammad b. al-Qāsim precious items, money, and jewels, but he accepted nothing except a comprehensive Quran that belonged to Ibn Ṭāhir. ʿAbdullah b. Ṭāhir was pleased because Muḥammad used it for his studies.

A revolutionary figure like Muḥammad and a revolt like his indicate that the missionary movement never ceased its path and remained steadfast in its principles. These characteristics are consistent throughout the revolutionary movements led by the missionary cause.

During the strained political climate from the time of Imam al-Jawād, peace be upon him, the revolutionary movements took on a distinctive nature. The situation of the missionary movement during Imam al-Jawād's time was favorable. If the most difficult period for the missionary movement was during the days of Imam Mūsā b. Jaʿfar

(ʻa), then the best times were during Imam al-Jawād's era. It is perhaps for this reason that the tradition narrated by Ibn Asbāṭ and ʿAbbād b. Ismāʿīl states:

"We were with Imam al-Riḍā (ʻa) in Minā when Abū Jaʿfar (ʻa) was brought before us. We said, 'Is this the blessed newborn?' He replied, 'Yes, this is the newborn who brings more blessings to Islam than any other people.'"[1]

Abū Yaḥyā al-Ṣanʿānī narrated: "I was with Abū al-Ḥassan (ʻa) when his son Abū Jaʿfar (ʻa) was brought in as a child. He said, 'This is the newborn who brings more blessings to our followers than any other.'"

The blessing that the missionary movement received from the birth of Imam al-Jawād (ʻa) was not just the reduction of terrorism and political oppression. More importantly, it solidified the movement's message in terms of belief, thought, politics, and jurisprudence.

---

1. Al-Majlisiī, *Biḥār al-Anwār,* vol. 50, p. 23.

Chapter Five

His Character and Virtues

A) The Generous and Noble

Our ninth Imam was titled "Generous" due to his well-known generosity that flowed abundantly, covering both plains and mountains, just as light spreads over the plains.

Here are some stories of his generosity:

His practical program: He received a letter from his father from Khūrāsān when he was about six years old. The letter included the following:

“I ask you by my right upon you, do not enter or exit except through the main door. When you ride, carry gold and silver with you, and do not let anyone ask you without giving to them. If any of your uncles ask you to honor them, do not give them less than fifty dinars, and the rest is up to you. If any of your aunts ask, do not give them less than twenty-five dinars, and the rest is up to you. I want Allah to elevate you, so spend without fearing poverty from the One who holds the Throne."

It was narrated that he received a large shipment of valuable goods. When the carrier informed him that it was stolen on the way, he wrote back in his own handwriting: "Our lives and our wealth are among the gifts and entrusted loans from Allah. He grants joy and delight with what He gives and takes back in reward and reckoning. Whoever allows their grief to overpower their patience loses their reward. We seek refuge with Allah from that."[1]

One of his companions, who owed a debt to the Imam, entered upon him and said: "May I be your ransom, please relieve me of ten thousand dirhams, for I have spent them."Abū Jaʿfar (peace be upon him) said to him: "You are relieved," and the matter was settled.[2]

B) His Asceticism and Piety

A narrator reports: "I performed Hajj during the time of Abū Jaʿfar (peace be upon him) and came to him in Medina. When I entered the house, Abū Jaʿfar (peace be upon him) was standing on a platform without a cushion to sit on. A servant brought a prayer mat and laid it for him. He sat down, and when I saw him, I was awe-struck and dazed. I attempted to climb the platform without using the steps, but he pointed to the place of the steps, so I climbed, greeted him, and he returned the greeting. He extended his hand to me; I took it, kissed it, placed it on my face, and he seated me by his side. I held his hand due to my amazement, and he let me to hold it until I calmed down."

He received people at a ceremony held in his honor during the Ḥajj season, attended by many scholars from Iraq, Egypt, and Ḥijāz. He greeted them wearing two shirts, a turban with two tassels, and sandals.

Abū Hāshim narrates: "Abū Jaʿfar (peace be upon him) once gave me three hundred dinars and instructed me to deliver them to one of his cousins. He told me, 'He will tell you to direct him to someone from whom he can buy goods. So, direct him.' I delivered the dinars and told him, 'O Abū Hashim, direct me to someone from whom I can buy goods,' and I did."[3]

One of his companions, named Ibn Ḥadīd, said: "I went with a

---

1. *Tuḥaf al-ʿUqūl,* p. 339.

2. *Biḥār al-Anwār,* vol. 50, p. 105.

3. *Biḥār al-Anwār,* vol. 50, p. 41, second edition.

group of pilgrims, and we were robbed on the way. When I entered Medina, I met Abū Ja'far (peace be upon him) on the road and went to his house. I informed him of what had happened to us, and he provided me with clothes and gave me dinars, instructing me to distribute them among my companions according to what they had lost. I distributed them, and they matched exactly what had been lost, no more, no less."

Another narrator says: "I went to Abū Ja'far (peace be upon him) on Eid day and complained to him about my difficult circumstances. He lifted the prayer mat, took a gold ingot from the soil, and gave it to me. I took it to the market, and it weighed sixteen mithqals."[1]

'Umar ibn Rayyān said: "The caliph Ma'mūn tried to involve Abū Ja'far (peace be upon him) in corrupt activities to diminish his dignity and respect among the people. He tried every possible means, but nothing worked. When he wanted to marry his daughter to him, he brought a hundred of the most beautiful maids, each holding a tray of jewels, to welcome Abū Ja'far (peace be upon him) as he sat in the bridal chamber. The Imam did not pay attention to them. There was a man named Mukhāriq, a singer with a loud voice and a long beard. Ma'mūn called him and said: 'If there is anything worldly about him, I will take care of it for you.' He sat in front of Abū Ja'far ('a) and sang loudly, gathering people around. When he sang for a while without the Imam paying attention, he finally raised his head and said: 'Fear Allah, O man with the beard!' Mukhāriq's instrument and hand fell, and he was never able to use them until he died."[2]

One of his father's companions, who was still young, brought some toys for children to play with. When he came and stood before him, he was not allowed to sit. He threw what he had brought in front of him, which angered the Imam, who said: 'We were not created for this.'"

---

1. *Biḥār al-Anwār,* vol. 50, p. 49.

2. *Manāqib Āl Abī Ṭālib,* vol. 4, p. 396.

C) His Knowledge and Culture:

We have previously discussed the knowledge of the Imams (peace be upon them) in my book on the life of Imam Jaʿfar al-Ṣādiq (ʻa), who spread the knowledge of the Ahl al-Bayt (ʻa) to the East and West. We explained the concept of the Imams' knowledge of hidden matters. Nevertheless, I find it necessary to delve here into the vast knowledge of Imam al-Jawād (ʻa) and his culture, which stemmed from an inspired heart and a strong soul.

It has been widely narrated that he informed people of what was on their minds and what would happen to them in the future. This does not mean that the Imams possess knowledge of the unseen, but rather that they are connected to Allah, the Almighty, either through divine inspiration or through the Prophet (s). They acquire their knowledge directly, whereas other people obtain their knowledge through senses and experiences.

If modern experiments have proven the existence of the sixth sense in some individuals, it becomes easier for us to believe that Allah can bestow certain individuals with such abilities. Moreover, believing in Allah's power and capability to do everything without exception leads one to accept all possibilities if it is proven that Allah has willed it.

It was narrated that the governor of Mecca and Medina, Faraj al-Ruʿajī, who was an opponent of the Ahl al-Bayt, once said to Abū Jaʿfar (ʻa): "Your followers claim that you know the weight of every drop of the Tigris River." At that time, they were standing on the bank of the Tigris. The Imam (peace be upon him) replied: "Can Allah bestow such knowledge upon a mosquito from His creation or not?" The narrator said that Faraj replied: "Yes, He can." The Imam then said: "I am more honorable in the sight of Allah than a mosquito and most of His creation."

Indeed, the doubt arising from questioning Allah's power is weaker than the doubt in the brightness of the sun. However, skepticism remains valid when it concerns a person claiming this high position, which cannot be accepted without scrutiny and examination. But if it concerns the family of the Prophet (s), doubt vanishes after knowing that each Imam was the most knowledgeable of their time in all matters since they inherited the spiritual leadership. This was true for the Prophet (s) and all his successors (‘a).

It is sufficient to know that Imam al-Jawād (‘a) was once asked thirty thousand questions in a single gathering, and he answered them all at the age of eight or nine. At the age of sixteen, he attended a meeting with Caliph Maʾmūn and debated with the chief judge, completely confounding him. Given that Maʾmūn was known as the most knowledgeable of the Abbasid caliphs in the sciences of his time, and seeing his reverence for Ibn al-Riḍā (peace be upon him) in previous accounts, we understand the divine nature and quality of his knowledge.

Here are some narrations that highlight the knowledge of Imam al-Jawād (peace be upon him):

1. Umayyah b. ʿAlī said: "I was with Abū al-Ḥassan (‘a) in Mecca the year he performed Ḥajj. He then went to Khurāsān with Abū Jaʿfar (‘a). Abū al-Ḥassan (‘a) was bidding farewell to the Kaʿba, and after finishing his circumambulation, he went to the Maqām (Station of Ibrahim) and prayed. Abū Jaʿfar (‘a) was carried on the neck of Muwaffaq as he circumambulated. Abū Jaʿfar (‘a) then went to the Ḥijr (of Ismāʿīl) and sat there for a long time. Muwaffaq said to him: 'Rise, may I be your ransom.' Abū Jaʿfar (‘a) replied: 'I do not wish to leave this place unless Allah wills.' Sorrow was evident on his face. Muwaffaq went to Abū al-Ḥassan (‘a) and informed him. Abū al-Ḥassan (‘a) came to Abū Jaʿfar (‘a) and said: 'Rise, my beloved.' He replied: 'I do not wish to leave this place.' Abū al-Ḥassan (‘a) said: 'Yes, my beloved, rise.' Then he said: 'How can I rise when I have bid the house farewell and will not return to it?' Abū al-Ḥassan (‘a) replied: 'Rise, my beloved,' and he rose with him."

2. It is narrated that Yaḥyā ibn Aktham, the chief judge during al-Maʾmūn's era, who was suspected of having converted to Shīʿa in the

last days of his life, said: "While I was circumambulating the grave of the Messenger of Allah (s), I saw Muḥammad b. ʿAlī al-Riḍā (ʻa) circumambulating it. I engaged him in a discussion on various matters, and he answered all my questions. I said to him: 'By Allah, I wish to ask you one question, but I am embarrassed to do so.' He said to me: 'I will inform you before you ask me. You wish to ask about the Imam.' I replied: 'By Allah, yes.' He said: 'Then it is me.' I said: 'Give me a sign.' He had a staff in his hand, and it spoke, saying: 'He is my master, the Imam of this age, and the proof (*ḥujja*).' "[1]

3. It is narrated that Maʾmūn passed by Ibn al-Riḍā (peace be upon him) while he was among some children. They all fled except him. Maʾmūn said: 'Bring him to me.' He asked: 'Why did you not flee with the rest of the children?' He replied: 'I have committed no sin to flee from it, and the road was not narrow for me to make way for you. Go where you wish.' Maʾmūn asked: 'Who are you?' He replied: 'I am Muḥammad b. ʿAlī b. Mūsā b. Jaʿfar b. Muḥammad b. ʿAlī b. al-Husayn b. ʿAlī b. Abī Ṭālib (ʻa).' Maʾmūn asked: 'What do you know?' He replied: 'Ask me about the news of the heavens.' Maʾmūn asked: 'What do you have from the news of the heavens?' He replied: 'Indeed, O Commander of the Faithful, my father told me, from my ancestors, from the Prophet (s), from Gabriel, from the Lord of the Worlds that He said: "Between the sky and the air is a turbulent sea with waves, containing green-bellied and speckle-backed creatures. The kings catch them with grey falcons to test scholars.' Maʾmūn said: 'You have spoken the truth, your father has spoken the truth, your grandfather has spoken the truth, and your Lord has spoken the truth.' He then let him mount his steed, and later married him to his daughter, Umm al-Faḍl."[2]

4. It is narrated that a phlebotomist was called by Imam Abū Jaʿfar (ʻa) the second during Maʾmūn's time. The Imam asked him to draw

---

1. *Al-Kāfī,* vol. 1, p. 353.

2. *Biḥār al-Anwār,* vol. 50, p. 56.

blood from the "radiant vein." The phlebotomist said: "I do not know this vein, my master, and I have never heard of it." The Imam showed it to him. When he made a puncture in the vein, yellow fluid flowed until the basin was filled. The Imam then said: "Stop it," and ordered the basin to be emptied. He then said: "Release it," and less fluid came out. He then said: "Bind it now." After binding it, the Imam ordered a hundred dinars to be given to him. The phlebotomist took them and went to Yūḥannā ibn Bakhtīshūʿ, narrating what had happened. Yūḥannā said: "By Allah, I have never heard of this vein in my medical studies. But there is a certain bishop who has been around for many years. Let us go to him, if he knows, well and good, otherwise, we will not find anyone else who does." They went to the bishop and narrated the story to him. The bishop pondered for a while and then said: "This man is either a prophet or from the progeny of a prophet."

These stories and others demonstrate the extraordinary knowledge of the Imams, which should not surprise us. Allah chooses to bestow His knowledge, power, and wisdom on individuals whose hearts He has tested, purified, and made exemplary.

D) Imam al-Jawād (ʻa) and Fabricated Narrations

It is narrated that when Maʾmūn married his daughter Umm al-Faḍl to Abū Jaʿfar (ʻa), one day he was in a gathering with the Imam, while Yaḥyā b. Aktham, and a large group of people were also present. Yaḥyā b. Aktham asked him: "What do you say, O son of the Messenger of Allah, about the report that says Gabriel descended to the Messenger of Allah (s) and said: 'O Muḥammad, Allah Almighty sends you His greetings and says to you: Ask Abū Bakr if he is pleased with Me, for I am pleased with him?'"

Abū Jaʿfar (ʻa) replied: "I do not deny the rank of Abū Bakr, but it is incumbent upon the one who reports this to match it with what the Messenger of Allah (s) said during the Farewell Pilgrimage:

'Many falsehoods have been attributed to me, and they will

increase. So, whoever deliberately lies about me, let him prepare his seat in Hell. When you receive a narration, present it against the Book of Allah and my Sunnah. If it agrees with the Book of Allah and my Sunnah, accept it, and if it contradicts the Book of Allah and my Sunnah, reject it.'

This narration does not agree with the Book of Allah, as Allah says:

'Indeed, We created man and We know what his soul whispers to him, and We are closer to him than his jugular vein.'[1]

According to the verse Allah is closer to man than his own jugular vein, so how is it possible that He is not aware of Abū Bakr's feeling and had to send Jibrail to ascertain if Abū Bakr was pleased with Allah!? Is it even logical to claim of Allah's approval from Abū Bakr or Allah's misunderstanding of Abū Bakr's feelings?

Then Yaḥyā b. Aktham said: "It is also narrated that Abū Bakr and ʿUmar are like Gabriel and Michael on earth."

The Imam replied: "This too must be examined, because Gabriel and Michael are two honored angels of Allah who never disobeyed Him and have never deviated from His command for a moment. However, Abū Bakr and ʿUmar associated partners with Allah before they embraced Islam and spent most of their lives in disbelief. It is therefore impossible to compare them to the angels."

Yaḥyā said: "It is also narrated that they are the masters of the elderly in Paradise. What do you say about this?"

The Imam said: "This narration is also impossible because all the inhabitants of Paradise will be youthful, and there will be no elderly among them. This narration was fabricated by the Umayyads to contradict the report in which the Messenger of Allah (s) said about Ḥassan and Ḥusayn that they are the masters of the youth in Paradise."

Yaḥyā b. Aktham said: "It is also said that ʿUmar is the light of the inhabitants of Paradise."

1. Quran 50:16

The Imam replied: "This claim is implausible because in paradise, for in Paradise there are the close angels of Allah, Adam, Muḥammad, and all the prophets and messengers. Hence, how can paradise fail to illuminate by their presence but by the light of ʿUmar?

Yaḥyā said: "It is also narrated that tranquility speaks through the tongue of ʿUmar."

The Imam replied: "Abū Bakr was better than ʿUmar, yet he climbed the pulpit and said, 'I have a Satan who misleads me. Whenever you witness me straying, return me to the straight path.'"

Yaḥyā said: "It is also narrated that the Prophet, peace be upon him and his family, said: 'If I had not been raised as a Prophet, surely ʿUmar would have been raised as one.'"

The Imam replied: "The Book of Allah is more truthful than this narration, as Allah says in His Book:

'And when We took from the Prophets their covenant, and from you and from Noah.'[1]

It is clear from this verse that the Almighty took a covenant of the prophets, so how could He change His covenant? None of the prophets engaged in shirk even for a blink of an eye. How can Allah raise someone as a prophet who spent most of his life associating partners with the Almighty? The beloved Prophet (s) also said: 'I was raised as a Prophet when Adam was between a soul and a body (before he was created.'"

Yaḥyā b. Aktham said: "It is also narrated that the Prophet (s) said: 'Whenever revelation was delayed, I feared it had descended upon the family of al-Khaṭṭāb.'"

The Imam replied: "This claim is inconceivable as the Prophet (s) would never doubt his own prophethood. Allah Almighty says:

'Allah chooses messengers from among angels and men. Indeed,

1. Quran 33:7

Allah is Hearing and Seeing.'[1]

How could the prophethood be transferred from the one Allah chose to someone who associated partners with Him?"

Yaḥyā b. Aktham said: "It is also narrated that the Prophet (s) said: 'If punishment were to descend, none would be saved except ʿUmar.'"

The Imam replied: "This too is impossible. Allah says:

'But Allah would not punish them while you are among them, and Allah would not punish them while they seek forgiveness.'[2]

Allah has informed that He will not punish anyone as long as the Messenger of Allah (s) is among them and as long as they seek forgiveness."[3]

E) I am Muḥammad

It is narrated that Imam al-Jawād (ʻa) was brought to the Mosque of the Messenger of Allah (s) after the death of his father, while he was still a child. He approached the pulpit and ascended one step, then spoke, saying:

"I am Muḥammad, the son of al-Riḍā. I am al-Jawād. I am the knower of the genealogies of people in the loins. I know your secrets and what you outwardly manifest, and what you are going to. This is knowledge granted to us by the Creator of all creation, from before the existence of the heavens and the earth, and after their extinction. If it were not for the overwhelming support of falsehood, the dominance of the people of error, and the rebellion of the doubters, I would have said something that would astonish the first and the last generations."

Then he placed his noble hand on his mouth and said: "O

1. Quran 22:75

2. Quran 8:33

3. *Biḥār al-Anwār,* vol. 50, p. 3, second edition.

Muḥammad, be silent as your forefathers were silent before you."

And in this destined measure, we praise Allah Almighty, send blessings upon His Prophet and the Infallibles from his family, and greet them with peace.

Made in the USA
Columbia, SC
13 September 2024

41653393R00035